R[eason] of the Rhyme

Gift copy to Joan & Mike

and Other Poems

by
Robert L. Laumeyer

Best wishes
Robert L. Laumeyer

Romance of the Rhyme

Copyright © 2004 by Robert L. Laumeyer

All rights reserved under International and Pan-American copyright conventions. No part of this book may be reproduced, stored in a retrieval system or transmitted in any form, electronic, mechanical, or by other means, without written permission of the author.

Library of Congress
Cataloging in Publication Data

ISBN 0-7951-0828-1

Reprinted by:
Moore Graphics
13415 W. Westgate Drive
Surprise, AZ 85374
623-972-8161

Foreword

Why Another Book?

If you feed a stray dog
He will stay at your home
If you praise a poet
He will write you a poem.

If at an author's work
You take a pleasant look,
Then buy some of his work,
He'll write another book.

Where Flowers Grow

As you read this small book
I would like you to know;
It is from dirt and manure
That pretty flowers grow.

This Book

I wanted this book perfect.
And I tried my very best.
Alas dear reader I fear
It came out much like the rest.

Some poems may give you a laugh,
Others may be, "food for thought."
Just do not expect too much,
It was a small book you bought.

Dedication

This book is dedicated to my grandchildren. Presently these are: Anne and Katherine Runkel, Alexander, Kathleen, and Robert O'Leary, Thomas Miner and Amanda Laumeyer. See page 109.

There is a special dedication to any one who becomes my grandchild after this book goes to press.

My wish for my grandchildren is that they have the wit and time to enjoy the romance of the rhyme of many poets.

I leave a special memory for grandson Charles Miner 1995 -2000.

> In time, in Poet's heaven
> May we all live the perfect rhyme,
> Where everything is beauty
> And there is love in every line.

I thank my wife, of over 50 years, Kathleen McGlynn Laumeyer, for helping me prepare this book.

Table of Contents

Administrator's Prayer 84
Afterthought 71
Almost. 44
America Under Attack. 67
American Independence. 68
American Taxpayer. 70
An American Conservative 69
Baseball 2001. 46
Believe 14
Boomers 87
Brave and Free. 65
Christmas Eve 52
Christmas Prayer 48
Christmas Spirit 49
Circles. 89
Consent 64
Conservative American. 69
Cowboy Poetry. 103, 104, 105
Dad and Dad's Lessons 21
Death of a Soldier. 63
Del Webb's Paradise Lost 80
Dichotomy. 90
Discontent. 11
Dissent 64
Dogs of War 63
Empty Words 18
Endless Trail. 17
Father's Day. 22
Father's Grave 101
Fly South 28
Friends 26
Future Poets. 96

Gardener's Creed	93
Gardener's Prayer	92
Golden Love Sonnet 1953-2003	37
Golden Sonnet	31
Golden Tale	33-34
Happy Birthday Wife	74
Happy New Year	53
Hate Vendors	102
Havre on the Highline	40
His Mother	58
Honesty Today	102
Hooked	24
Humor	83
I Heard The Carollers	85
In a Used Book Store	41
Infinity	19
Integrity	26
Learn	75
Learning	98
Long Shadows	106
Love the Irish	55
Luck of the Draw	23
Magic and Magic Desk	20
Marriage Advice to My Son	31
Mary's Old Oak Desk	51
Migration Time	39
Miner's Cabin	13
Mother's Gift of Love	58
Mother's Love	59
Mother's Peace	99
Motherhood	99
My Blessings	86
My Love-My Bride	36
My Mother's Love	57

My Mother's Tea	16
My Size	79
My Yule Log	50
Never Too Old	53
Nostalgia	85
Not Alone	12
Obituary of a Thinking Friend	19
"03" Opportunity	55
Our Golden Love	33
Paddy's Day	56
Perfect Poem	32
Plea of the Embryo	60
Poet's Fate	97
Poets for Peace	61
Poet's Prayer	10
Political Advice	66
Portly Poet	82
Price of Youth	76
Prince of Peace	48
Prose and Poetry	79
Pursuit	44
Renaissance	95
Romance	22
Romance Maker	107
Romance of the Rhyme	9
Romance of Youth	11
Romantic Promise	73
Same Sex Marriage	101
Self	43
Sleep in Quiet	67
Stand Tall	45
Stone Is the Thing	81
Sun City Valentine	32
Sun City Valentine's Day	30

Sun City Winter. 29
Sun City Youth 38
Sun City's Sadness 27
Sunset Poem 35
Talent and Common Sense 47
Talent God 78
Taxing Memories 71
Teachers. 42
Teachers Stand Tall 42
The Lonely Man's Prayer 15
The Old Desk Speaks 75
The New Year. 54
The Search 72-73
The Search for Youth 77
The Second Time Around. 25
The Truth is Hard to Tell. 65
Thought. 46
Thoughts of an Infidel. 94
To Mary. 51
U.S.A. Thanksgiving. 60
Understand. 91
Valentine's Day 2003 62
Valentine's Fire. 30
Wearing of the Green. 86
Wooden Axe. 100
Written in Stone 88
Your Best 45
Your Talents 27
Zest of Rhyme 108

Romance of the Rhyme

All my life I've been a dreamer
Some of my dreams have been sublime.
Somehow always my heart did quicken
Exposed to the romance of the rhyme.

When my life was most difficult
And my true self I had to find,
I would look to favorite poems
To feel the romance of the rhyme.

So come along with me my friend
And spend a little of your time.
If you are very fortunate,
You may find romance in the rhyme.

Epilogue

Books are worlds within themselves
A universe can be held on wooden shelves.
Poems are music in the air
The ageless dreams of those who care.

Romance books are best
To tell the reality of man;
For dreams are his essence
Though they may not be his plan.

Robert L. Laumeyer

Poet's Prayer

Oh God, give me the talent
To put great thoughts in each line.
Let my meter come out perfect
My chosen words always rhyme.

Let me so entrance the reader
He sees with my inner sight.
Let my verse overwhelm him
So he loves each poem I write.

Then God give me energy
To produce the perfect book,
Where I find a masterpiece
On every page, I look.

God, if you choose not to do
Any of these things above;
Just let me keep on writing
The poetry, that I love.

Epilogue

In time, in poet's heaven,
May I live the perfect rhyme,
Where everything is beauty
And there's love in every line.

Romance of Youth

The wail of the train's whistle
Is the song of the life untried.
I yearn to feel the wonder
Of that new exciting ride.

I long for the thrill to find,
Where this train is taking me,
Feel again the exuberance
Of the unknown, untried, and free.

Be the adventurous youth,
Of endless energy and hope
Not knowing what the fates hold,
But knowing the youth will cope.

Learn again sharp new pleasures,
Now blunt or dulled by time.
Recreate a youthful life
Relive, Romance of the Rhyme

Discontent

The young boy yearns to become a grown man,
To the youth, adults have exciting ways.
The adults fantasize about their youth,
Praise the mythical life in "The Good Old Days."
Every age has their time of discontent
We know the old wonder, where the years went.

Robert L. Laumeyer

Not Alone

Prologue

Knowing her granddad lived alone,
The granddaughter was a little sad.
So grandfather wrote for her this poem,
Telling her what books meant to his home.

Not Alone

Oh, he does not live alone.
He lives in a house with books,
And he has brilliant friends
On every shelf he looks.

They tell him their special thoughts
Through essay, fiction, or poem.
That's why he likes his friends
And keeps them in his home.

They are there when he needs them.
More lasting than what's heard.
If he forgets a statement
They can tell him word for word.

They're never untrue to him
They don't ask him for a thing.
He loves them on the shelf
In hand, great pleasure they bring.

Oh, he does not live alone.
He lives in a house with books.
And he has brilliant friends
On every shelf he looks.

Romance of the Rhyme

Miner's Cabin
On the Lazy L Ranch

Old, alone on the mountain ridge,
Are remains of the miner's home,
What hopes and dreams are buried here
And are his bones, beneath the stone?

Lonely hikers may see the ruins
But will they hear "his" siren call?
"Oh, leave the safety of the path
Come find my gold, and claim it all."

Climbing to the cabin remains
They see what he saw long ago,
What grandeur was the miner's view
With the river winding down below.

Many will stay on man's known road
And not seek for the golden ore.
It's easier to walk the traveled path
Than to climb where eagles soar.

Poets may take the miner's chance
For they live for moments of romance.

Robert L. Laumeyer

Believe

Believe in your self
God made you sublime.
It's your job to think
"Success will be mine."

Know the man who claims
This job I can't do!
Always will be right
Be sure he's not you.

He who does, is one
Who thinks that he can.
Be it write a book
Or a great race ran.

Do your very best,
Whatever your task.
That's all anyone
You, or God should ask.

Epilogue

Know you can fail
And yet not a failure be.
When a leaf falls.
It does not kill a tree.

Romance of the Rhyme

The Lonely Man's Prayer

He was long alone in his home
Living among the rocks and trees.
His music a coyote's howling
His company a mountain breeze.

Resting on his step he looked
At the night's bright display of stars.
Those candles of night, wondrous light
Made him forget, his drunks and bars.

Entranced he saw his childhood home
And his mother who taught him love.
She had told him about her God,
With her spirit he gazed above.

Reminiscing in the cool night air
He dreamed this lonely man's prayer.

"Are you there and do you care?
Do you have room for me?
I'm lost, the smallest needle
In the forest's largest tree.

How can I know? Will you show
That you have room for more?
I am small, lost on a shelf
In the world's largest store.

Are you one, to whom I count
Or do you know of me?
I'm but a grain of fine sand
Lying under the sea.

Are you there and do you care?
Do you have room for me?
I'm just a lonely soul
Awaiting your decree."

Robert L. Laumeyer

My Mother's Tea

Oh, somewhere high up above,
Well behind the brightest star,
I hear my mother calling
Telling where Dad and she are.

They are somewhere high above,
Far out in infinite space.
I see my Mother's eyes shine.
Almost feel her warm embrace.

The stars are the tiny cups,
That she is setting up for tea.
I "feel" her make that motion,
"Come sit and talk, you and me."

Her smile tells me death is good
And that God is mostly love.
She tells me not to hurry,
But come see them up above.

I know somewhere out in space
From where she has beckoned me,
That with her sway with her God,
I will make it to her tea.

Endless Trail

Prologue

An old poet who was shy on school
Felt learned poets may find him a fool.
He knew his rhymes were good, his poems true
Yet he was unsure—would his syntax do?
A well read man read his work, found it fine
He replied to him with this rhyme.

Endless Trail

There are many places to learn
The public school is surely one.
Good teachers are helpful coaches,
Aids, when the knowledge race is run.

Some young move on a slower path,
They may hit dark spots on the way.
Faster move the lucky children,
Whose parents taught them every day.

Many teachers have no degrees,
Mothers often are of the best,
Fathers showing young how to work,
Helped many pass life's hard test.

There is no ribbon finish line
Life's hope should be for learning more;
He who thinks he's reached the end
Is either dead or he's a bore.

He who goes the farthest in life's knowledge book.
Should not be faulted, for the path he took.

Robert L. Laumeyer

Empty Words

Prologue

Work's a treasure, it's sold by the pound.
Words are given away by the ton.
Loquacious people are still talking,
While the world's work is being done.

Empty Words

Too often you've found, when you heard,
"When it is all said and done."
You heard a lot of empty words,
But did not see any work begun.

The doers of the work express
Their thoughts about talkers quite well.
They refer to empty words as,
"Used hay from the bull corral."

Epilogue I

Learn that when you are in a race
And find you cannot run, then walk,
You will get to the end slowly,
But you'll never get there by talk.

Epilogue II

"That talk is cheap," You often hear,
The supply's too great, to be held dear.

Romance of the Rhyme

Obituary of a Thinking Friend

Ken T.

The bright flashes of color
With red, orange, and purple hue,
Weaves the cloth that makes our lives
A patch quilt of ones, we once knew.

The very fabric of our being
Is woven from different strings.
The more unique a person is
The brighter the thread he brings.

We find in the patterns of life
Some strange colors will not blend.
The deceased saw unique colors.
I was proud to call him friend.

If there is a thinker's heaven
Where new thoughts are greeted with song,
And old ideas are questioned
That's where my friend does belong.

Infinity

Oh, there are people out there,
Who know stuff that I don't know.
It was that way when I came.
It'll be that way when I go.

I thought I'd learned a lot,
But my knowledge store is poor.
For each fact that I've learned
There's at least a thousand more.

Robert L. Laumeyer

Magic Desk

To some it looked like an old worn desk,
But to the owner it looked a prize.
Her grandfather had given it to her.
And told her that it held a big surprise.

Grandfather said "It is a magic desk;
With it's power "You can create a poem."
He told her "That these great powers were
Even greater than Harry Potter's stone."

Now granddaughter knew her grandpa didn't lie,
But she wondered could her desk really write?
She would look for the magic tomorrow,
She had too much homework for tonight.

She studied hard, then she slept a little,
For her mind could hold no more mundane fact,
Too much arithmetic, too much spelling,
Her mind slept, it dreamed a poem intact.

Magic

There is magic in the air,
And it's magic that you own.
If you sit and study long
It will help you write a poem.

Grandpa wanted you to know
There's real magic in your head
And if you try hard enough
You will thrill, at what you said!

Dad

We hear so much of Mother
And so little about the Dad
We begin to wonder were
Immaculate conceptions had?

Dads don't love us any less
They just have a different way.
Their lessons about hard work
Once learned will forever stay.

Dads need to be hard and strong
To provide what their children need,
Lessons about honesty
And how to avoid evil greed.

I know I am prejudiced
For "strong" a man looks to a lad.
How thankful I am God gave me
A wonderful man for a dad.

Dad's Lessons

Deal from the top
And palm no card
Honesty is easy
Deceit is what's hard.

Play your hand well
For that is you.
It's not in the plan
For one to play two.

Robert L. Laumeyer

Father's Day

Long in the hospital he stayed awake
When a strange metamorphosis he had.
A young lover he'd gone to the hospital,
He came out a proud, caring dad.
He felt the urge to shout, to laugh, to pray;
Tumultuous feelings "his" first Father's Day.

Romance

My mirror through which I see the past
Is cloudy, has chips, and a crack.
The mirror has some clear, bright spots
That bring some of the good times back.

Some of the good events stand clear,
Poorer deeds are covered with haze;
But the older my mirror grows.
The more there are of hidden days.

Memory's mirror keeps getting worse.
Events are harder to keep straight.
I now have more things to forget.
Accept this, for an old man's fate.

Of the bright spots that stand out clear,
Some are of a long-ago lass.
Somehow old loves can look the best
When seen in a worn, foggy glass.

Romance of the Rhyme

Luck of the Draw

To prepare them for the life
Most expect to be their lot;
Youth are taught to do the right
And to avoid what is not.

Their parents, churches and schools
Teach them a stern conduct code,
That they find is very hard
To follow on life's long road.

But most of the time, most do
What as youngsters they were taught,
And then if things go awry
They feel cheated and distraught.

An old gambler once told me.
"Always play the best I could.
But know that being lucky,
Was better than being good."

Epilogue

Oh Maker of all mankind
I love beauty, thought, and pluck;
But for my life's companion
Please give me "Lady Luck!"

Robert L. Laumeyer

Hooked

He took a granddaughter fishing,
To teach her the fisherman's art.
Even when the fish weren't biting.
He could feel her nibble his heart.

They fished the cold, clear waters
Of a pretty Montana stream.
The more they fished together.
He found the more that she did mean.

Casting, wading, with her fly rod.
Showing enthusiasm and joy.
She reminded him of Grampa.
Who he fished with, when a boy.

The more times he took her fishing.
He, now playing grandfather's part,
They more he could feel her nibble.
Then she set the hook in his heart.

He lives in a moving circle.
Where time gives him a different role.
To find the scene wherein he fits.
For him, and all, a worthy goal.

See page 110

The Second Time Around

Born on a spinning planet,
We rode a merry-go-round,
When blessed with our children
Many new pleasures did abound.

The children grew and left us,
New homes of their own they found.
Then the Great God of Rebirth
Gave a second time around.

The generation growing
Is less work, more time for fun.
Our life's work behind us now,
We are glad that race is run.

The brass ring is ours to hold
To enjoy another ride.
Life's different the second round
With the grandkids by our side.

Epilogue

There is yet a tale to tell
About this free ride of gold.
We see what our parents saw,
When we thought that they were old.

Robert L. Laumeyer

Friends

All want friends to give hope
When they are in bad times.
These friends may be great thoughts
Told in near-perfect rhymes.

Greater yet is man's need
For friends when things are good.
His joy he wants to share,
When life goes like it should.

He can't share happiness
With even the best tome,
And a whole library
Can not applaud his poem.

Friends are more than just words.
Man needs man to share joy.
His friends are life's substance.
His books but a great toy.

Epilogue

The best of life depends
On sharing it with friends.

Integrity

A poor man may have but his integrity
But no honest man is ever totally poor.
The man of integrity possesses a quality;
That he, God, and all mankind can adore.

Romance of the Rhyme

Sun City's Sadness

There is a sadness in Sun City
That the realtors do not let you know.
You meet friendly retired people
But you find, in time, these friends must go.

Rock cutters, poets, and silversmiths
Their friendship we shall never forget.
We know their inspiration lingers.
We pray, beyond, new clubs they'll beget.

When we go to that not so distant shore,
And join them in their heavenly flock.
We hope to find them working silver
Or grinding on a heavenly rock.

Poetic friends we hold are working,
To write thoughts of heavenly delight.
From these now quiet bards, we expect,
Powerful new poems, with great insight.

Oh, friends, who we have loved before,
We long to see you beyond that door.

Your Talents

Remember when you sing
Your retirement song;
That if you do nothing,
You may be doing wrong.

Robert L. Laumeyer

Fly South

The rivers I fished, now have banks of gold.
The story of autumn is being retold.
Evening air now has a cold, fresh, biting sting.
A clear warning to all, what winter will bring.

There are imperfect "vees" forming in the sky
Made by noisy, anxious geese flocking to fly.
They have left the arctic ahead of the storm,
Seeking a winter home that's comfortably warm.

Now I too feel this relentless urge to go,
To avoid the coming cold and winter snow.
Friends of your old tired bodies take pity,
Come to a great warm place called Sun City.

Epilogue

I need no more of ice, cold, or snow.
Oh, of winter I have had my fill!
Now to the sun and warmth I go.
Where I watch beautiful roses grow.

Sun City Winter

From the mountains of Montana
To the warm desert plains below,
This senior Montana native
Was driven by the cold and snow.

To the heartland of the summer,
To the land of sand and warm sun,
This old Montana poet goes
When he knows winter has begun.

To the land of golf and hobbies,
Where the retired go to play,
This fugitive from the cold goes
And enjoys his winter stay.

This old Montana traveler thinks
In all the "lower forty-eight,
That for its warm winter climate
Sun City should be rated great!

Robert L. Laumeyer

Sun City Valentine's Day

Two old lovers
Walking hand in hand;
Living in peace
In Webb's promised land.

The setting sun
Marks their day most done;
Old love's stronger
Than when it was young.

A show of love
All can understand;
Two old lovers
Walking hand in hand.

Valentine's Fire

It is beautiful as the sunset
And as strong as the rising tide,
It is as endless as the longing
That makes man pursue his bride.

Fortunate are the happy ones
Who have a love that doesn't tire,
Let's all celebrate Lover's Day,
Enjoy their Valentine's fire.

Romance of the Rhyme

Golden Sonnet

How do you say, "I love you",
To one fifty years your bride?
What words have you not used
To keep your love by your side.

What can you give her, that is new
After eighteen thousand days?
How about you try a kiss!
And give her a little praise?

The God of love has a rule
That true love shall not grow old,
For the lucky ones he makes
Anniversaries of gold!

Tell her once more of your love.
Then both thank the God above.

The author and his wife
were married August 31,
1953 in Miles City, Montana.

See page 111

Marriage Advice to My Son

Remember if you have told
Your loving mate something twice,
The third time you should try flowers,
They'll fare better, than more advice.

Robert L. Laumeyer

Sun City Valentine

On Valentine's Day we write
Poems or verse on what we hold dear.
We read of love of country,
But little of what we have here.

We've palms that reach toward God,
Golf courses green with winter rye,
Lakes that deny the desert,
And deep blue Arizona sky.

Well kept homes in rock filled yards
Wide boulevard with room to spare.
Old lovers walking hand-in-hand,
Showing us all how much they care.

Our days end with an artist's touch,
Painted canvas with orange and gold.
The valentine that I will write:
"I love you, City of the Old".

Perfect Poem

The perfect poem I was going to write,
When my wife said "Best come to bed tonight".
I put down my pen and went to my bed
Now you may wonder what I never said.

Our Golden Love

Oh, we had lots of fun and laughter,
We also had some sorrow and tears.
We found it took a lot of loving
To be married fifty golden years.

Thank the God who gave us quick young minds
And healthy grown bodies, lithe and strong;
The luck to love and health to survive.
We were blessed to hear our golden song.

Beloved, we've earned just part of the praise.
The Lord has cared for us all of these days.

Golden Tale

Prologue

It was over a half century ago
That in college these two young people met.
He thought she was the prettiest ever.
Thanks to the God of Romance he thinks so yet.

It was a very different era
Religion and parents taught, date and wait.
These two young believed, when the time was right,
They would meet and marry their life long mate.

Mostly it worked the way they were taught,
And it still works out for them very well.
That is why in the journal of their life,
They love and have a golden tale to tell.

Robert L. Laumeyer

Golden Tale

Two short stories were edited to one,
That August day, in an old Montana town.
There stood two loving, enchanted spirits,
He wore a brown suit, she was in a white gown.

Each story was just in its beginning,
But now they both prayed for a common end
They had no idea, what their book would hold,
On their honesty, each knew they could depend.

The God of love and laughter took command,
And created much new romance for their book.
It became a tale of a family
The editors found, four new authors it took.

Fifty years of editing has been done.
Much has been said of what was, and
what was not.
The two short stories of so long ago.
Make a book, yet each kept a separate plot.

Epilogue

The golden message they would like to leave,
From their odyssey of long ago past.
"With the God of Romance in your corner
When you both work hard, true love can last and last!"

See pages 111 and 112

Romance of the Rhyme

Sunset Poem

There are dark blue mountains
Framed in a dull orange sky
Large gray geese go flying by.

A distant silent jet
Leaving a long glowing trail
Shadows grow, night will prevail.

Mature golf course walkers
Are walking towards their home,
Many not seeing the poem.

The sunsets in Sun City
Make a colorful display
Creating new poems each day.

Robert L. Laumeyer

My Love – My Bride

In a world of cynics, that scoff and scorn
We danced and courted, our love was born.
Love, a sparkling star, romantic as night
A thrilling bonding, filled with delight.

Long we've been married, love still has its sway.
Your sparkle still brightens my dim pathway.
Five decades seeing your impish smile.
Pray! Gods of love, give me yet awhile.

Some things I've learned, outlived our youth
Our love is as permanent as the truth.
In a world of indulgence and quick gains
Happy am I, our youthful love remains.

Scientists, math experts, nor poets know
What can make some loves for fifty years grow.
Other loves they've seen blaze, then quickly die.
How lucky in love, were my bride and I.

Romance of the Rhyme

Golden Love Sonnet 1953 - 2003

I gave you pearls the day we were wed.
Today I give you a golden chain.
Only the God who gave us our love
Knows how long our earth love will remain.

The pearls were a token of my love,
Each bead had a story to be told.
Now love, let this golden chain's glitter
Shine on those good times, we love to hold.

Eighteen thousand days and even more
You have brought a glow into my heart.
After fifty years "love of my life"
It's still much too soon for us to part.

Let's pray our souls drift off together
So no lonesome one is left behind
Then in eternal space may there be
Another golden life for us to find.

Ah my beloved, today fifty years we've been wed
Pray, the best part of our love poem is still unsaid.

Robert L. Laumeyer

Sun City Youth

To D. M. M.

There may be youth in the heart
Even when age is in the bone.
Some may have a space within
Where youth's made a permanent home.

True, old bodies must wear out,
But the spirit within may stay young.
The spirit of the old gray man,
May be the boy's, from which he's sprung:

When you see an old woman,
With sore legs, but a youthful grin;
Remember that there may be
A laughing teenager within.

Some who in a walker depart,
May display the youth in their heart.

Romance of the Rhyme

Migration Time

We think we hear the whir of wings
Of the snowbirds going home,
But we find what we really hear
Is this valley merchant's poem.

"Oh fly safely birds of the snow
We want you all back, you see,
For you provide the beautiful green
Of our valley money tree.

"Oh snowbirds of the tundra land
Now you flee from summer sun.
Enjoy yourself in a cooler clime,
But come back when summer's done.

"It's true we condemn your driving
And speak ill about your ways;
But know, when it comes to money
We bless your shopping days!"

Robert L. Laumeyer

Havre on the Highline *

It's Havre on the Highline
Then the home of N.M.C*.
It's where our loves came together
Long ago, for you and me.

The century was half over
And we were so very young,
Our childhood was now over
Our adulthood not begun.

The first day that I met you
Your beauty struck me numb.
I could barely speak to you
I feared you thought me dumb.

We didn't fall, we grew in love,
In those care free happy days.
Took time to know each other,
And learned each other's ways.

The first time I kissed you,
Gave me my life's greatest thrill.
It's now over fifty years
And your kisses do so still.

It's Havre on the highline
Then the home of N.M.C.
It's a very special place
Where you gave your love to me.

Epilogue

Fifty years we have been wed,
Sweetheart, how kind time has been.
For when I look at you now
I still see what I saw then!

*Highline - A Montana plateau
*N.M.C. Northern Montana College

In a Used Book Store

A True Story

My moment of fame came, in an old book store.
I've a lot of books, but I still look for more.
I found Eliot's book named "The Waste Land,"
And Fitzgerald's Picture on Poems by Khayyam.

I was pleased with the price, three dollars each.
Suddenly I saw a book just past my reach!
It was my first born, "Poems of the Hunter's Song."
With these great authors did my first book belong?

The shoppers around me heard a gasp of glee
A four dollar price tag I could clearly see.
A dollar more than Eliot was about right,
But outpricing Omar! I questioned my sight!

I found in time common sense must have its say!
I paid nine dollars for Edna St. Vincent Millay!

*This took place in
"Aunt Bonnie's Used Books"
Helena, Montana, July 14, 2003*

Robert L. Laumeyer

Teachers

The shadows that the teachers cast,
Grow longer as their days recede.
Those that taught the rambunctious youth,
Did not know, if they did succeed.

As these teachers move to darkness
The light they provided can glow.
They pray that the seeds they planted,
In fertile fields, now will grow.

The generations yet unborn
And youth that are now being taught;
Can thank dedicated teachers
For the progress of human thought.

When into the abyss teachers go,
Know it was their work that let man grow.

Teachers Stand Tall

Bold and kind are worthy teachers of youth,
Tough they are, those purveyors of truth;
Farmers of grey matter who plant the seeds
Of the crops that civilization needs.

Teachers, top professionals, bask in the sun;
Shedding light on youth whose quest has just begun.
Good teachers believe, knowledge all can share.
The great ones never admit this error.

Why?

BECAUSE THEY CARE!

Self

Oh, what is honor,
Fame or even health,
If you can not feel
Good about yourself?

It makes no difference.
What honors you've won,
If you don't feel good
About number one.

Give yourself a break,
If you can't reach high.
Praise yourself a bit,
Just because you try.

Always remember
At every day's end,
Treat yourself as good
As you treat a friend.

Robert L. Laumeyer

Almost

A full bodied woman stretching,
Trying to reach a high shelf,
Urgent, urge to reach out and touch,
But firm control of one's self.

A large bright red apple setting
In a shaft of brilliant light,
The thought that it's a painting
Stops you from taking a bite.

Poems scattered on a large desk,
Verses wherever you look.
Here's the substance and fulfillment,
But not the pages of a book

Close we are to the 'touch and taste"
And to the books that are not born.
"ALMOST" such a colossal waste,
No great trees, just an acorn.

Pursuit

The pretty young intern
And the little pill,
Can they bring the pleasure
Of the youth's lustful will?

Oh, man has long searched
For his elusive youth.
It is gone forever
Is a relentless truth.

Your Best

When your book of verse is closed,
And your life goes out with the tide.
When the great librarian above
Goes over your work to decide,
If it meets the heavenly standard.
Pray you have earned a "He tried."

When the final grade is given
To all who have taken the test,
Ultimate teacher will promote
The ones who have given their best.

Stand Tall

Our lives are but a drop,
In the sea of endless time.
Our poems are but commas,
In a giant book of rhyme.

Still our ego tells us
We are the very core.
There is a lot of clay,
But we are golden ore.

Know, your spirit is your all!
Show that spirit, you stand tall!

Robert L. Laumeyer

Thought

Thinking does not empty thought's cup.
That container's a strange device.
The sips or drafts that are taken,
The thought God replaces them twice.

Unused, the cup of thought runs dry,
Potential changed into air.
Evaporated by doctrine,
The shunned cup of thought goes bare.

Cowards may shun to take thought's drink,
To be unsure makes egos shrink.

Baseball 2001
Jewel of the Desert

The desert breeds determination
Its offspring are resolute and strong.
They crave the world's greatest respect
For they want all to know they belong.
In a world of terrorism and war
They did not let freedom's light grow dim.
They called to the team in the desert;
"Hone your skills, work hard, play hard and win.
The intellectuals told them
It's just a game, boys and men play,
But when the World Series came around
Their souls knew "The Great American Way."
With the dreams of boys and the work of men.
They were determined to win the plaques.
They defeated the greatest dynasty of them all;
Now they are "the Mighty Diamondbacks."

Talent and Common Sense

In the confused world of the mind
Much of who we are has been taught.
Some earned knowledge in life's school
Others from college it was bought.

Two great things that all desire,
But no one is sure one can teach,
Are common sense and talent, "Gems."
Are these beyond the teacher's reach?

Some hold teaching will dull these gems.
Some think college these gems enhance.
The preponderance of evidence
Shows that ownership is pure chance.

How can we test for common sense,
What kind of a test could that be?
That is not very hard my friend.
Give an "A" if they think like Thee.

Talent will be a harder test.
You'll look for what did talent make?
Test the quality, is it good,
Or did "you", find the product fake?

Robert L. Laumeyer

Prince of Peace

The stir of Christmas is in the air.
The excitement of our youth is there
Mystical thoughts, goodwill, will prevail,
And the Prince of Peace the world will hail.

Oh, Prince of Peace, show people your will.
Teach them, other men they should not kill.
Tell the leaders, who teach men to hate,
That they'll find a lock on heaven's gate.

Please, this Christmas, the world, with peace bless.
Teach us all, love of man to profess.
When love for our fellow man we gain,
Then, you, oh, Prince of Peace will reign.

Christmas Prayer

Oh, listen to the angels.
Enjoy their loud trumpet call.
Pray to know on Christmas
There is a child in us all.

Then dream the thoughts of a child
And enjoy their love of play.
Know there's a child in us all
Reborn every Christmas day.

Find you are never too old
To enjoy Christmas's cheer.
I pray you carry that joy
Throughout the coming New Year.

Christmas Spirit

The Christmas spirit is not time or place.
It is a delightful burst of joy.
It can exist in an old man's heart,
Much as it did when he was a boy.

A shiny dump truck under a tree,
A Christmas present of long ago.
It was a very different world then.
It was a Christmas with cold and snow.

Still, the power of that Christmas magic,
Brings a joy that's hard to understand.
It need not be in a world of white.
It can be a land of sun and sand.

That Christmas happiness still lives on,
Much as it did in that dump truck toy.
The magic is not of time or place,
It's a spark of God, in man or boy.

Oh, if love and justice would kindle,
That bright God-like spark into a flame;
Then instead of Christmas once a year,
Eternally peace and joy would remain.

Pray the spirit of Christmas lives on!
And hate and war are forever gone.

A MERRY CHRISTMAS WISH

Robert L. Laumeyer

My Yule Log

The elf of Christmas looked
Into my window to see,
Not just who I was today
But who I had been at three.

He saw life as a log's end.
Saw the growth rings and the core.
Knew each ring was still in me,
Looked deeper to find more.

Elf saw my first Christmases.
Saw all of my childhood fun.
Then he looked at outer rings,
Saw where old age had begun.

Elf read all rings to the last,
The one you can see today
He closed his magic notebook,
And on spirit wings flew away.

Took his notes to headquarters,
Each ring, a person to recreate
The summation who I was,
Showed who I was young and late.

The committee saw the whole,
Saw all the rings who still "are."
Their verdict was, "Send to him
A magical Christmas star."

"A Star of magical light
Show him the great life he had.
Show this grumpy grandfather
In him lives a joyful lad."

"When this old man sees himself
Made from all he has been,
He'll learn the best game of all is
(Christmas, Remember When!)"

Romance of the Rhyme

Mary's Old Oak Desk

There's a lot of fancy glitter
Sold in many modern store.
Mary went to a thrift shop,
And found something worth much more.

Scratches, dents, and bad varnish
Made very good wood look bad.
She saw the quality there
And took it home to her Dad.

He worked hard on the desk,
Now she can show it with pride,
And tell her friends, "You should know
What counts is what's inside."

A truth of men, desks, and books,
Don't judge quality by looks.

To Mary

Enjoy the quality
You saw this desk had,
And think loving thoughts
Of your "Dear Old Dad."

Merry Christmas 2003

Robert L. Laumeyer

Christmas Eve

It was a Christmas Eve in Sun City
With dark blue mountains and dull orange sky.
There was nostalgia for Christmases past,
Childhood Christmases are last to die.

In the Midwest, the Northwest, North and West
Sun City people had lived when young,
Now they "saw" their homes, their parents, their friends.
Where their first Christmases had begun.

Sleigh bells, greetings, and laughter could be "heard"
And children singing songs in the night.
Dolls and toys gone, except from memory
Now seen in Christmas's magic light.

Christmas peace descended on Sun City
As the Christmas eve grew darker still.
This cheerful thought invaded people's souls.
"Oh! Christmas Lives And it Always Will"

Never Too Old

Prologue

Know on Christmas Day the world revives,
That's why the youth, in your heart survives.

Never Too Old

You are never too old for Christmas
Although Santa may fade away.
You're never too old to wish a friend
A very happy Christmas Day.

You must take the World for what it is,
Learn to keep the good, the bad dismiss.
Getting old has problems a plenty,
But you're never too old for Christmas.

Happy New Year

"Prosperous year to you
We hope you make a lot."
Is a wish made by those
Who think wealth's what you've got.

The wiser people know,
If wealth is to be real;
It can't be what you own,
It must be what you feel.

My New Year's wish for you
Is for Peace and good Cheer.
May it be with you now
And last throughout the year.

Robert L. Laumeyer

The New Year

New Years is a new start,
For every saint and sage.
The poetic guys too
Get to start a new page.

May your new start be fun.
Your work make new pages glow.
When the pages are joined,
May your book "success" grow.

Of all the new beginnings
Old December did beget,
May the one born this year
Be the greatest one yet!

On the top of my new page
I'll write for you this poem.
"May the coming year find you
Safe and happy in your home."

"03" Opportunity

Oh, it's a new beginning,
For all a shining clean start.
A hope for a better tomorrow,
It's a glow within our heart.

The "02" year is over.
It's mistakes we can't undo.
Now it's time to look ahead,
See how much better we can do.

With lots of work and effort,
We have made it to "03".
Now let's work for tomorrow,
And see how good it can be.

Love the Irish

It is easy to love the Irish
With their blarney and romantic song.
The American people love the Irish.
Even when the Irish don't get along.

It is easy to love the Irish.
With just their smile, most hearts they win.
Little chance do simple mortals have
When there's a Leprechaun's soul within.

It is easy to love the Irish.
The uninhibited way they play,
Makes Americans love them more,
Especially on St. Patrick's Day.

Robert L. Laumeyer

Paddy's Day   Butte, Montana

Paddy O' was an Irish lad,
And he loved his strong Irish brew.
He read of the Butte copper mines
And wondered just what he could do.

He dreamed of a job well paid
Where he could live a free life.
He wanted children and a home
With his fair colleen for a wife.

He went to Montana to dig,
Deep underground the copper ore.
Soon they built new, his Irish Pub.
He longed for home even more.

At first he wanted to get rich,
Then go back to his Irish home;
But the rich pay from the copper
Told him this world could be his own.

He sent for his Irish colleen.
Built the churches where they would pray.
This new land has kept Paddy's best
His dreams, and St. Patrick's Day.

Romance of the Rhyme

My Mother's Love

Prologue

A mother's love is the seed
That fosters the child's loving deed.

My Mother's Love

I've memories of the past
Of my mother's loving heart.
Two parents cared for me
Mother had a unique part.

Loving warmth against the cold
Comfort from being alone,
Fond childhood memories glow,
"Mother" in my boyhood home.

She to nurture me with love,
And amuse me with her song.
When she would hold me close,
I knew nothing could go wrong.

Mother, builder of courage,
Shaper of my thoughts of right,
Through turbulent growing years
You were my strong, lighthouse light.

Epilogue

When in life, someone does good,
Know his mother, knew he could.

Robert L. Laumeyer

His Mother

As rain drops feed the growing creek,
And as many creeks make the brook,
Her letters spell out various words.
Then in time the words make his book.

Thus his mother loved her child
Fulfilling the details of God's plan,
Nurtured him along the way,
Saw him become a caring man.

This Mother's love he never lost,
Though he often hid it away.
Now it rushes into his heart
Whenever he thinks of Mother's Day.

Mother's Gift of Love

The good Priest related stories about
Unearned and unrestricted love.
A gift sent to earthlings down below
From the almighty God high above.

My first reaction was disbelief
It seemed love of this kind couldn't be;
But then my thoughts wandered back
Recalling my Mother's love for me.

Mother's Love

To protect, care for, and feed her young
Is the mother's natural emotion.
She shows a harsh uncaring world
The strength and beauty of devotion.

Her love blazes as a beacon
And it shines far out, bright and true.
When you are lost or confused;
This is your mother's gift to you.

Oh! Mother's love is a timeless thing,
It appears that it's written in stone.
It's not dependent on what you've done
It is your shield from being alone.

When you count your blessings from above,
Know that one great gift, is Mother's love!

Robert L. Laumeyer

Plea of the Embryo

No taxation without representation,
Was the battle cry of a proud new nation.

Now from the unborn, we hear this woeful plea.
"Tax yourselves, pay your debts, don't leave them to me."

"You know we can't rebel, we are yet unborn.
Please show us your honesty, not your greed and scorn.
A proud new nation should show that it values truth.
Not pass on its debts to its unborn youth."

"Leave us a country that is proud and debt free;
That's a true legacy of democracy."

U.S.A. Thanksgiving

We have a "Thank you God" feeling
We pray will last throughout the year.
It surrounds our Thanksgiving day.
Knowing we're safe, well fed, and here.

We thank the ones who went before,
For the bountifulness they grew.
We thank farmers of today,
That our stores of food they renew.

We are thankful some keep us safe
And we thank those that give us love.
We're thankful we're in a country,
Where we can thank the God above.

Romance of the Rhyme

Poets for Peace

Oh! Beware the tree of hate
Is growing a deadly plum.
Beware, beware, don't you know
Where the fire of war comes from?

Evil men searched and found
Blossoms they could pollinate.
These men used prejudice
To spread the pollen of hate.

Snarled on the trunk of hate
Grow enormous weeds of greed.
Now beware! Do you not know
On what the wars of men feed?

Men of power came and used
Fear to fertilize the ground.
They made a dangerous garden
Where their armies now abound.

Religious sophists turned
Man's humanity into naught,
Thus it is in sacred names
Bloody wars can now be fought.

Hate, greed, fear, and sophist's fruit,
Soiled much of mankind's past.
Weed out plants that grow this fruit,
Plant fairness, that peace may last.

Let poets take up the task,
And chop down the tree of hate,
Then show a weary people
That war need not be man's fate.

Robert L. Laumeyer

Valentine's Day 2003

Oh it is hard to write of love,
In a world engulfed by hate.
It seems February Fourteenth
Is to be just another date.

The power of evil and greed,
Make mockery of a day for love.
I wonder what the "Father' thinks,
When he looks down from high above.

He who made the turtle and hare,
Cannot think there's only one right.
Why did he make the sun for day,
And stars and the moon for the night.

Oh, write no love poem for the day
When world leaders demand we kill.
Strange those who would teach us of God.
Know so little about His will.

Romance of the Rhyme

Death of a Soldier

Does it matter
That a uniform he wore;
That youth, too young
To know the horror of war?

Is his young life
Somehow held to be less dear;
Because he's past
School's graduation year?

Do we know youth
Are, our most precious jewel?
How dare some men
Dress them to be a war's tool?

Epilogue

Start From Where You Are!
If the Supreme Court reversed itself,
And said "Count the votes, instead."
Would the law of ex post facto,
Make any of the victims, less dead?

Dogs of War

Our dogs of war, have tender butts,
For they have not been through the fray.
When they were called to duty
Safety said, "Go the OTHER way!"

Robert L. Laumeyer

Consent

The preemptive strike
Is not a new thing.
Herod ordered one
When he was the king.

When once ensnared by
The Seducer, "Power."
Man's common decency
Ambition may devour.

Rulers, rule by different codes,
Their bond "power is dear."
Man's moral opinions,
Are a force that they fear.

Are innocent those who
Perform the ruler's way,
When by doing his work
Own thoughts of right they slay?

Dissent

The right of free man's honest dissent
Is given by God, not government sent.
A foolish child may hold a bird so tight
He destroys forever that bird's flight.

Learn powerful men, led by fear or greed
Can destroy the choices that free men need.
Know that man can destroy what he holds dear;
If he is a slave, to a coward's fear.

Romance of the Rhyme

The Truth Is Hard to Tell

First we fight an expensive war
And then we search for the reason.
Some did pretend before the war
That to question it was treason.

Some demand we praise the outcome
Claim terrorism's been struck a blow.
The frustrating historical fact.
"Was this war needed?" We'll not know.

One thing we know, is some men lie
And in war we know, men will die.

Brave and Free

Long I have praised "The Bill of Rights."
Amendments that our freedoms depend.
I wonder as I read them again.
As stated, will our leaders defend?

In these times of terrorism and war.
Will they modify these rights in fear.
Then in zealous acts to protect us.
Lose, what our forefathers held most dear?

Robert L. Laumeyer

Political Advice

When the harsh unblemished truth hurts you,
And your excuses are pretty thin.
Know there's a political tactic
That is known as the great media spin.

When being honest does not persuade,
When with logic and reason you try;
It is time to learn "New Politics."
Tell all who'll listen, a great big lie.

If you do not have an honest face,
Try big business and learn from crooks.
Just remember to lie really big
Then with distain for truth "Cook the books."

Give the politicians their big share,
For then, the lawmen, they will take care.

Epilogue

If you want to live by what's true
You may lose wealth and elections too.
But know on the penny you see the face
Of a man who served and didn't disgrace.

America Under Attack

The heat from the friction of ideas
Produced a gigantic funeral pyre.
The materials of the Trade Center
Were reduced to but rubble and fire.

The Saints and Sinners died, side by side.
Comingled, their ashes were interred.
No one can or will separate them
Until the deity's voice is heard.

Bold, but misguided courage, displayed,
In such a monstrous, vicious plot,
By those that were indoctrinated
Instead of, thinking, being taught.

May the fires of this fearful crime,
Burn out the core of those who chose hate.
May all the suffering they caused
From this pain a kinder world create.

Let all the people of the world see
The deeds that hate does attract,
Then let the love of man and justice,
Rise from the fires of this attack.

Sleep in Quiet

Let Peace descend, where we let Omar lie,
End the misery that's now above his grave,
Then wine, not guns, the people may buy.
Let all men choose their way before they die.

Robert L. Laumeyer

American Independence

Oh, we may curse our president
And his cabinet members, too
We can fault the mighty Senate
And damn whatever the House may do.

Some may condemn the government
They need not hold back what they say.
They are using a great freedom
Protected by the U.S.A.

We have the right to curse and damn
But at least one thing we should praise,
There'll be no dungeon awaiting us,
As there may have been in former days.

Americans, stand around our flag.
Let us to our creator pray.
"We have not made it perfect yet
But thanks, Lord, for the U.S.A."

Let our enemies be aware
That to fear we will not bend.
We criticize our government,
But our country we will defend!

An axiom learned about democracy
Is that freedom can never, forever be free!

Conservative American
To R.F.M.

Prologue

It is true about poor old conservative Bob.
U.S. politics for him is a hard job.
All of his life frugal government he did praise,
His party got control, then took a big raise!

An American Conservative

The U.S. Conservative
In truth is a dinosaur.
Best look closely at him now
For you may see him no more.

He sought conservative friends.
People who state's rights defend.
A government where income
Determines what it will spend.

A political party
That sees church and state have grown,
Yet knows our constitution
States, that each must stand alone.

He searched for a party
As dinosaurs sought a mate.
Compatibility not found,
Extinction to be his fate.

Robert L. Laumeyer

American Taxpayer

It's time to do taxes again
It seems like I barely got done.
Now the more years I acquire
The faster new ones are begun.

How hard the forms, high the cost
My anger rose, how hard this task.
My money and this hard work too,
This seemed just too much to ask!

From numbers and forms this thought grew:
"How many would be glad to pay
Much more than this if they could live
In our wonderful U.S.A?"

Back to work on the hard tough forms
I will do the best that I can.
When done, I'll thank the God above
I WAS BORN AN AMERICAN!

Romance of the Rhyme

Taxing Memories

Recording my annual income
Is a very trying event.
I have to find how in it came,
And then find out how it was spent.

I always try to be honest,
I was taught it is wrong to cheat.
But oh "Wizard of the tax code,."
A legal loophole would be neat.

I am not un-American
I feel the patriotic touch,
But please, Mr. Tax Collector
I can't believe I owe that much.

Oh what a cold world it seems to be
When it is one for you and two for me.

Afterthought

If any of these poems got you to think
Then you have filled my heart with glee.
The objective was to inspire thought
Not to make you agree with me.

Robert L. Laumeyer

The Search

A ghost town with long forgotten mines,
Scars where once homes and dreams had grown,
Closet-like homes, held castle plans
But more of poor, than wealth was known.

You can feel the vibrance of the mines,
But you can see no miners now.
They came to find sudden wealth
Not hoe or plant or use a plow.

Off to the next mine or heartbreak,
Miners "knew" the next place would bring gold!
They left piles of waste rock and hope,
Sad memories the ghost towns hold.

Yet among this rot and decay
You see a tiny crocus rise.
This small purple flower glimmers
The beauty of hope never dies.

The crumbled rock and fallen roofs
Show you something of what life means.
Be it gold, or a perfect verse,
Man was born to pursue his dreams.

Men of rhyme spend money and time
Just to hear one another speak.
Is it fame or a golden verse
That they go to conventions to seek?

The Search
(continued)

Tons of rock the miners moved
To get bits of the golden ore.
Man still treasures its brilliant shine.
Will poets work contribute more?

Will our poets leave but rubble?
Fame is fleeting and plaques will mold.
Will their poems be rotting logs
OR WILL THEY LEAVE A VERSE OF GOLD?

Romantic Promise

To my descendents and to my friends,
I want you all to know;
The best of life on romance depends.
That is why the search never ends.

Robert L. Laumeyer

Happy Birthday Wife

Oh, remember when we were young
How we praised each birthday year?
They were milestones of progress,
Bringing our adulthood ever near.

Oh, remember the excitement,
That we had to be coming grown?
When most of life was yet ahead,
Now, dear friend most of our life is known.

As your candles in number grow,
Some exuberance may grow less.
I pray the candles brightly glow
And show you greater happiness.

As your life's story is being told,
May each birthday be a bead of gold!

Epilogue

Oh, one part I know well,
my love
As the years go by, I love
you still.
There's welcome warmth
in my heart,
Assuring me I always will.

Romance of the Rhyme

The Old Desk Speaks

More than a hundred years ago
I came from oak trees, tall and true.
When made, I was young and pretty,
Had a deep and lustrous hue.

I was built with love and pride.
I was prepared to give good use.
In time, hard times came upon me.
I suffered neglect and abuse.

I was scratched, nicked, stained,
Leg broken and joints were shaken.
Damaged, to a garage I went,
In time to a thrift store taken.

With great care I've been restored
Again I'm proud to look my best.
Know that for 100 years
My quality has withstood the test.

Learn

The value of men, desks, and books,
Shouldn't be judged by outside looks.

Robert L. Laumeyer

Price of Youth

In a dream my memory went back
To life in the lost world of my past.
Again I was loved, by some now dead.
I had strong feelings this love would last.

Then my reason came to me and said,
"To you that world is forever lost,
You strove to live the life of today
Your life of former years was the cost."

Then in my dream, came a messenger
He spoke like an old and knowing sage.
He said, "I met the boy of your youth,
Told him the way he could stay that age."

"To stay the same age, you must be dead."
Were the words the philosopher said.

Romance of the Rhyme

The Search for Youth

Some have the will of a teenager
But a body that is soft and old.
To these old men, bottles and bottles
Of blue colored wistful hope is sold.

Most men thought they knew what they wanted.
But many learn that is not the truth,
For what they really wanted to buy
Was the strength and swagger of their youth.

But alas to stand tall
on Youth's great mountain
Pills are as futile as Florida's
lost fountain.

Robert L. Laumeyer

Talent God

Prologue

At a poetry reading,
I was bored by blank verse.
I began to wonder if
I would someday write worse.

Talent God

Into my bank account of talents
I thank you for every deposit you've made.
I have spent your gifts most lavishly.
It was that they'd go unused, I was most afraid.

Oh Granter of all gifts and talents,
You've enabled me to enjoy many a craft.
I have enjoyed writing all my life,
Please let me stop, before there's an overdraft.

Romance of the Rhyme

Prose and Poetry

It's true a little story
May dispel the darkest gloom.
Bring a warm and cheerful light
Into a cold and dark room.

For me a thing that's better,
Is a thoughtful, romantic poem.
It's romance can bring to me,
The heartfelt, warm love of home.

Somewhere out beyond my reach,
There exists a perfect rhyme.
Just my knowing that it's there,
Makes me feel it can be mine.

My Size

I went to see my doctor,
Lost time from retired day.
After many thumps and prods,
This is what he had to say:

"Just eat less, exercise more,
To aid good health, do your part!"
He handed me his Bible;
It was a height and weight chart.

I looked at the printed scale
And gave a triumphant snort.
"This does not say I'm too fat
It says I'm six inches short."

Robert L. Laumeyer

Prologue to Del Webb's Paradise Lost

In nineteen sixty, Sun City was a plan.
Dell Webb was a successful construction man

He put a lot of his money, work, and time,
To make some feel, retirement was sublime.

Sun's newspaper has a column called "Vent."
Here unsigned vituperations are sent.
To readers the problems may seem strange or small,
But the Daily News-Sun gives a voice to all.

Del Webb's Paradise Lost

Oh what a wise community this could be
If only age would cure tomfoolery.
It is sad, I see this is not the case,
Years are but flags marking the end of the race.

We see how some retirement years are spent
When we read the problems some want to vent.
One says "My neighbor's open garage is a sight,"
Another that garage sales start before daylight.

To some, real estate signs are a disgrace,
It makes one wonder how they bought their place.
Or how about this most infamous quote,
"My rec. card is mutilated when I vote!"

Oh what a great community this would be
If from trivial annoyances, we were free.

Romance of the Rhyme

Stone Is the Thing

We all love the glitter
Of shiny bows and string
But when the box is open
We know the stone's the thing.

Oh, platinum will shine
High karat gold will glow;
What stone is in the ring,
Is what girls want to know.

Ask the unmarried girl
"What really makes a ring?"
I will bet you a karat
She will say "The stone's the thing."

You know it's not silver
That will make her your own;
For in your heart you know
That she must have "THE STONE."

Life's customs you may want to mock;
But first my friend, give her "THE ROCK."

Robert L. Laumeyer

Prologue to Portly Poet From Montana

Out in western North Dakota
Where Roosevelt ran many a cow,
A French man built a packing plant
Then named the town after his frau.
Now in that quaint Medora town
Many a cowboy poet can be found.

Portly Poet From Montana

He's a portly poet from Montana.
He is sure not starving, we can see.
He hasn't ridden much the last fifty years,
Montana horses that big couldn't be.

He went out to that old Medora town
Just to read a little cowboy rhyme.
So just sit back and relax a little
I won't let him take up too much time.

We know that he sometimes gets too windy
When he piles it up a bit too high;
But forgive him please, he is from that land,
That's called by many, "The Big Sky"

Now he loves the tales that exaggerate,
And some say he tells them pretty well;
But in Medora overstatement's name,
Is, "Used hay from the bull corral."

Romance of the Rhyme

Humor

Prologue

I praised Poet Lombardi,*
Told her "Your poems are of the best."
She said, "My poems don't matter much,
All they are is a rhyming jest."

Humor

Humor is such a precious thing
For it gives to many some joy.
Don't ever belittle laughter
It is something all can enjoy.

My hat is off to the poet
Who can make a person smile.
Some doubt worth, of what makes one think
But all know humor is worthwhile.

Epilogue

In conclusion
I simply state,
Take courage, don't quake.
A being without a sense of humor
Did not mankind make!

*Doris Lombardi a Sun City deceased poet

Robert L. Laumeyer

A Poem for School Administrators Everywhere

Administrator's Prayer

Some administrators that I knew
Read my prayer for the makers of verse
They wondered if they couldn't have help
To cope with the administrators' curse.

They read the song of an old sinner
Found a prayer for a rounder too,
But nary a word about themselves,
This omission they felt would not do.

They read the "Lonely Man's Prayer"
Saw my poem "Embryos Have A Plea"
They formed a high brass committee
To requisition work from me.

"Surely we must be more worthy
Than the songs you write for sinners.
Come write a poem for us
We are education's winners."

They mandated "Write a poem to God
An appeal to give us our fair share."
Hard I worked but all I found was,
Administrators just don't have a prayer!

Nostalgia

Gnawing hunger in the soul
For a food that is no more.
Good memories of a life
That we have lived before.

A deep feeling of sadness
For the ones, we cannot see.
Silken bondage to the past
Without a wish to be free.

With thoughts of youth our memory plays,
In the mind exists, the good old days.

I Heard the Carollers

Boulder, Montana 1985

The bright reds and greens of Christmas wear,
And strong fresh voices on evening air,
Told me that the carollers were there.

Loudly they sang of their Christmas goal,
That peace and good will would fill our soul,
And that for Christmas the world would be whole.

The hope of youth and beauty of song,
Made me feel in God's love all belong,
And that man's love of Peace made us strong.

Now when I hear that of war or peace,
Men cannot decide,
I hear again the Carollers sing
And feel their peace inside.

Robert L. Laumeyer

My Blessings

Every Thanksgiving Day
My blessings I try to recall
The older that I grow,
The harder it becomes to list all!

When I try to pick out
Which of my many blessings are best
My dear wife, tops the list,
First there is wife! Then all the rest.

Epilogue

How good our God has been
To give us fifty years to spend

Wearing of the Green

It's time for corned beef and cabbage
And tankards of mint green beer.
The leprechauns are playing tricks
For St Patrick's Day is near.

The Irish gents are laughing
And the colleens are all aglow.
For this is an Irish holiday,
And they want the whole world to know.

Let the shamrocks grow a brighter green
Let the four leaf clover abound.
Then let all the world enjoy
The wit and luck the Irish have found.

Romance of the Rhyme

Boomers

Oh! Baby boomers
Know you have had your day.
It seemed forever
You boomers had the sway.

You chose the music
And you set the style.
To depression's kids
It seemed a long while.

But now you boomers
We have you by the hair.
We are your parents
Who you now, must take care.

When we leave this scene
And our stories are told,
You're no longer "hip"
For then you'll be "the old."

Epilogue

May you hunt hard for what you want,
For hunting is much of the fun.
May memories bring you pleasure
When all your hunting days are done.

Robert L. Laumeyer

Written in Stone

I dreamed a heavenly dream,
Saw parts of an eerie scene.
My free spirit was looking down,
Saw my dead body under ground.

What should the stone's engraving say?
Was the main topic of the day.
Some said, "write, POET on his stone,
In life he sought the perfect poem"

As a teacher he earned his keep,
So under that word let him sleep."
Philosopher," others cried,
"That would his thinking, best describe."

Flattered I was from what I heard,
But "spirit" sent down this more quiet word.
"From your lofty words men may shrink,
engrave." "HE TRIED TO MAKE MEN THINK."

Epilogue

Strange, how a dream could life's goal show.
I wanted men, to think, not "know."
Now awake, my life revived,
Thought, dead, deeds are judged

BEST STAY ALIVE!

Circles

Clouds in a winter sky
Wind driven, floating by,
Thoughts in an old gray head
Revealing poems unsaid.

Clouds nor thoughts know their end.
There's change ahead, depend
No more a cloudy day
Wind blew them all away.

Wait! I can see some white,
Another cloud's in sight.
When thoughts enter death's door,
Can they, too, again soar?

New life, of thought or cloud,
In circles is it allowed?

Robert L. Laumeyer

Dichotomy

We can see the shades of darkness
Our souls can hear a mournful call,
But something in us will not accept
A coming time that will end it all.

A time where there is no chance to change
The time of the last kiss, the last good night,
Opportunity gone forever
For that perfect poem we were to write.

We fear to travel to the unknown
A place where we've often tried to look.
Scary this road we travel alone
For all must go without friend or book.

Afraid to know is there a next home?
Mortal thought says all that starts must end.
We fear a "nothing' no love or poem
Enjoy the "NOW" it's all you can depend.

Brought forth from the chaos of thought
Checkered squares of bliss and blight
Our moments of exhilaration
Are intermingled with the dark of night.

A flow of morning light strikes our bed
Showing us an invincible plan,
An endless chain of lifeless motion.
Who dares hold less for thinking man?

Understand

Prologue

Oh what I can see, from where I stand
Is much more of life than I can understand.

Understand

What I have learned,
On my walk in this park,
Is that God may know,
But man's kept in the dark.

That what I can hear
From religion's high Priests,
Is less of God's thoughts,
Than his heavenly feasts.

I've held a grandchild,
Buried, Mother and Dad,
I've lived a full life.
I've been happy and sad.

Yes, what I have seen
From the places I've stood,
Was far more of life
Than what I understood.

Epilogue

Oh what I can see from where I stand
Is much more of life than I can understand.

Robert L. Laumeyer

Gardener's Prayer

I'm sorry "Master Gardener,"
You, who can make all things grow.
I have ignored your churches
I could not see what they know.

I cannot sing heavenly praise
For I do not know the songs.
When I die you may well find
I have done too many wrongs.

"Pious" may have all the rooms,
You may not have one to spare,
Remember I can garden,
Of your flowers I'll take care.

Please set aside a small spot
I'll make us a flower plot.

Epilogue

Oh God of supreme power
With the pious I may not feel at home.
Save for me a garden spot,
A pen, and place, where I can write a poem.

Gardener's Creed

A lowly garden is my church
I go there most every day.
I weed and feed, and water,
For that is my way to pray.

I don't need a holy book
That tells of a Christmas birth.
I plant my seed with great care
Then I watch the fertile earth.

Soon then my healthy plants grow,
In time begin to flower.
No need for a tomb to show
The resurrection power.

Oh! To see God's creation,
For a church I have no need.
I just go to my garden
And see the power of seed.

Epilogue

Life's great mystery we cannot understand.
Life wasn't made for mortals to know the plot.
We were all given a time and place to stand.
I have tried to show and explain my spot.

Robert L. Laumeyer

Thoughts of an Infidel

Oh, in this land of wait and wonder
I'm filled with religious treason.
I was not given the gift of faith.
I have but the burden of reason.

The religious tell me lack of faith,
Will lead many person's souls to doom.
My nature demands I think about,
What is on the dark side of the moon.

If in this curious world of wait,
Maker wanted all of us the same,
Why did he make the ant and the horse
Also why the mountain and the plain?

I will think for reason says I must,
Thinking tells me, His judgment is just.

Romance of the Rhyme

Renaissance

In an old soiled garden box
He found one dry shriveled bean.
He planted it with apathy,
After all, what could one seed mean?

It grew into a healthy plant,
Big green leaves and flowers of white.
Inevitably in fall
Came a cold, clear, moonlight night.

Now with sadness he went to view
The once beautiful plant he'd grown
Sadly he gathered brown dead pods,
Shelled, chaff to the wind was blown.

He scooped beans into his hand
Now forty, where he'd had but one.
Had he created brand-new life,
Or was all there, when he'd begun?

Dreaming he saw his grandchildren
In the bright new world of today.
Awake he saw his dried beans,
He thoughtfully put his seeds away.

He saw eternal life in his hand
Yet knowing, was beyond his reach.
The tiny grains of sand can't see
The great distances of the beach.

See page 110

Robert L. Laumeyer

Future Poets

When the romance for rhyme is fading
When the sky in the west is lighted in red,
Those who love to read good poetry
Must know, many dreams were left unsaid.

If past poets had greater talent,
Had they worked harder at their task,
Still they would not have accomplished,
All that the lords of poetry ask.

It is time you pick up the gauntlet
Accept the challenge to create art.
Who knows what great lines you may form
If you champion the Poet's part.

Learn, "Gems of Wisdom", may be found
Lying on unhallowed ground

Poet's Fate

Between real and imagination
In a world not awake or asleep,
There is a fuzzy never-land
Where our creative souls we keep.

We dream in this fantasy land,
Perfect things we expect to find,
As morning light hits our eyes
They exist, only in our mind.

Awake we'll not accept this fact,
To books of Poetry we flee.
We reread the old, ponder the new
But no perfection can we see.

Then our minds envision a book
Where each poem is exactly right.
With glee we seek paper and pen
But perfection flees when we write.

The rule to pursue, but yet fail,
Is decreed to be Poet's fate.
Romance of the rhymes may linger
The sought for perfection must wait.

Our new books of poems we've begun,
Even though we painfully know,
That the perfect verse will not come,
The fate of poets every one.

Robert L. Laumeyer

Learning

"Read"

Learn to read most carefully
Use a very candid eye.
Or in the poorly written
A great truth may fly on by.

It's fun to read the writer
Who can make his message flow.
But he who does not write well
May have facts that you should know.

"Listen"

The mind may want to wander
When the speaker is not fine.
Learn unique is the person
Who does not have one good line

Believe everyone out there
Knows some thing you have not heard
Teach your mind to follow him
And digest his every word.

For learning you have a good start,
When your eye and ear play their part.

Motherhood

Of all the things people do
Of all the jobs they've begun,
One stands above all the rest
That's the raising of the young.

So stand tall, you mothers all,
Who have cared for your young.
That is the greatest job now!
And has been since time begun.

Mother's Peace

Still in the night, I hear her,
Though long ago, she went away.
I can feel her, tuck me in,
While she teaches me to pray.

Time and place bring small change,
To one entranced in love.
I can still hear her soft voice
Coming to me from above.

Now I ask the creator,
"Give her the care, she gave me."
Then in her far promised land,
She'll be at peace eternally.

Robert L. Laumeyer

Wooden Axe

Prologue

On a mountain walk one morning
I found a weathered wooden toy.
I admired how well it was made,
Thought about a long ago joy.

Wooden Axe

On my walk under shady trees
Suddenly came a shifting breeze.
There exposed to my surprised sight
A child's toy, made for playful fight.

Among the needles of the pine
Lay a toy of a former time.
A small wooden axe made with care
Showing a love, that fathers share.

A father's love was on display
As under the tree that toy lay.
How long ago, did that man live
Who, for his son, had time to give?

A feeling of awe within me grew,
This man and son I felt I knew,
Because I too have known the fun
Of making toys for my son.

Epilogue

It was not just an axe on the ground,
But the brotherhood of man I found!

Father's Grave

As the sun set over his father's grave,
He heard the notes of a meadowlark song.
He was the only person there to hear
Because all the other mourners had gone.

His father's life had been a hard journey,
He struggled hard for the successes won.
As the sun set and the meadow lark sang,
This prayer was offered by his youngest son.

"God here lies a good man
Please provide him your best.
He worked hard in life
Yet still had time to jest."

As the meadow lark sang his song of joy,
Father and song, lived on in the boy.

Same Sex Marriage

Now about this same sex marriage thing
I really wonder, what is all the fuss?
I know I sure don't want to have one,
Even if church and state did bless us.

Epilogue

Let's lighten up a bit
And not by state's decree,
Try to enact new laws
So that all live like me.

Robert L. Laumeyer

Hate Vendors

The tongues of flame that burn freedom,
Are fed by charcoal blocks of hate.
Freedom we held so dear is gone
If intolerance is our fate.

News commentators can be ones
Who dispel news full of bias.
They love to act religious men
Teach their hate and act so pious.

Epilogue

If speech we choose to not regulate,
We can not stop those who peddle hate.
So let them speak, but ignore their lies,
Know over our land "Old Glory" flies

Honesty Today

An honest man must always say
That what he believes true today,
Even when it will contradict
His beliefs spoken yesterday.

Some people feel their thoughts so true
That in their life; they learn no new.
Most hope they learn along the way
Then their old words, would lie to you.

Epilogue

If it's consistency you yearn
Look for a man who does not learn.
If it is thinking you would cheer
Then expect different thoughts to hear.

Cowboy Poetry

Prologue

Now what is cowboy poetry
Some poetic friends ask of me?
How does it differ from the rest?
Is it true, or do they but jest?

Cowboy Poetry

It's the best way of telling stories,
For it is written in rhyming verse.
Cowboy Poets say just what they mean
To emphasize, they may even curse.

Cowboy poets create a rhythm
They hope you can feel in your soul.
To make the old West live again
Is every cowboy poet's goal.

You will know their verses when you hear them.
Their thoughts are of a former time.
It's tales of the romantic west
Told in the best old masculine rhyme.

It is well worth your while, to hear it live.
Go to a "Gathering" where their poems thrive.

Epilogue

Some of you may find there's more romance,
Hidden under a cowgirl's bonnet,
Than leading literary critics
Can find in a Shakespearean sonnet.

Robert L. Laumeyer

Cowboys of My Youth

Prologue

I was thinking of my youth
And the cowboys way back then.
I was just a little guy
Felt big! I was almost ten.

W.W. II had not begun
Always cowboys were for hire
Most of them would work short jobs
With a month's pay they'd retire.

These cowboys were carefree men
So their money didn't go far.
When broke, their employment office
Was the local friendly bar.

From the stories I heard them tell
I knew romance was their goal.
They would laugh and swear together
Their poems were kept in their soul.

If they knew rhymes, I think they did.
They thought ones not fit for a kid.

Romance of the Rhyme

Cowboys of My Youth

In the days of long ago
When I was so very young.
Cowboys were the mystery men
That Phonograph songs were sung.

I watched cowboys with awe
The way they would sit their mount.
Even if I heard of faults
With me, none of them would count.

I watched them roll a smoke
From their little Durham sack
I practiced on the "makins"
I found in the cowboy shack.

Oh! In my long ago youth
Cowboys could do most anything,
They could ride and rope and smoke

But

I never knew one to sing.

Epilogue

I know there were cowboys who sang
Some even played in the band.
But the cowboys I knew as a kid
Were ones that wore a different brand.

Robert L. Laumeyer

Long Shadows

This may be the end of my romance tale
For I see long shadows on my trail.
Life has been good to me, but with a flaw.
Most of what I've seen, I dreamed, not saw.

Books should end when the reader still wants more.
Trails should end before they become a bore.
Take time, to learn to love, and learn to dream,
You'll know what romance of the rhyme can mean.

When you've loved and dreamed and shown care,
Pray your thoughts of romance, the world will share.
If not, the loves and dreams are worthwhile still
For a dreamer of romance knows no fill.

Epilogue

My book of poetry I lay away.
The click of the switch marks the close of the day.
Alone in the dark, with time to think,
As if of life to take one long drink.

And savor the flavor, so eminently brewed,
For thought and reflection are life's food.
So eat, drink, and remember long
For thought is poetry and poetry is song.

Romance of the Rhyme

Romance Maker

Don't heed my fleeting cry to know.
I have a greater need to think.
If I had the fount of knowledge
I would forgo the urge to drink.

In your vast garden of creation
You gave me a mind for a hoe.
Surrounded by a forest of facts
I strive to make a flower grow.

Thank you for the opportunity
To plant, to hoe, to think, and to pray.
Thank you for the hoe you gave, and
For the love, I found along the way.

I didn't learn, the wonder or the why;
But thanks for the hoe and time to try.

Robert L. Laumeyer

Zest of Rhyme

As long as freedom loving man,
Is given hope, and thought, and time;
As long as fragile hearts can love,
There will be romance, told in rhyme

If man's hopes are turned to ashes,
And his thoughts held to be a crime;
There'll be a criminal out there,
Who'll create romance of the rhyme.

Man's longing has a resilience,
And over mountains it will climb;
For the essence of his being,
Is romance, boldly told in rhyme.

Epilogue

Alas, my friend, this book must end.
I hope some romance you did find.
On writers alone don't depend,
Your romance must spring from your mind.

Dedication

left, to top, to right
Robert O'Leary   Amanda Laumeyer   Anne Runkel
Alexander O'Leary   Katherine Runkel   Kathleen O'Leary
center - Thomas Miner

Hooked

Katie O'Leary

Tom Miner

Renaissance

Anne and Kate Runkel